PIANO VOCAL GUITAR

PENTATONIX

D0510705

ISBN 978-1-4950-5599-7

HAL•LEONARD®
CORPORATION

7777 W. BLUEMOUND RD. P.O. BOX 13819 MILWAUKEE, WI 53213

Visit Hal Leonard Online at
www.halleonard.com

PENTATONIX

AVI KAPLAN

KIRSTIN MALDONADO

SCOTT HOYING

MITCH GRASSI

KEVIN "K.O." OLUSOLA

NA NA NA

Words and Music by AVRIEL KAPLAN,
KEVIN OLUSOLA and TAYLOR PARKS

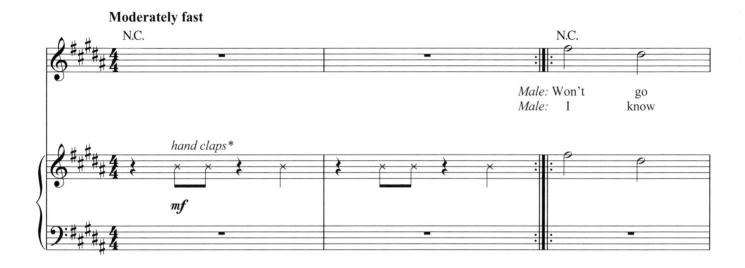

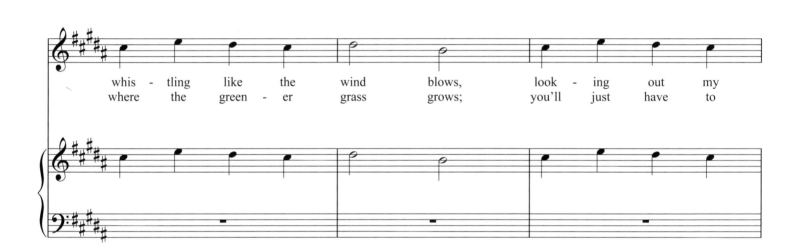

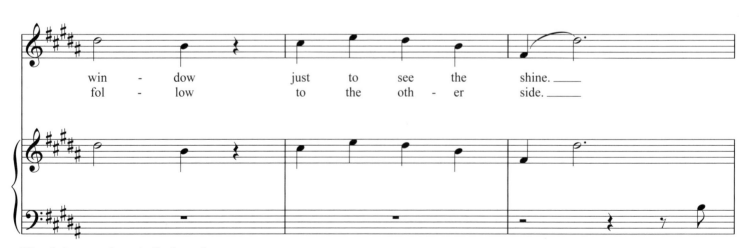

*Hand claps continue simile throughout song.

Females: Don't it feel like: (Na, na, na, na, na, na, na, na, na,

na, na, na, na, na). Don't it feel like: (Na, na, na, na, na,

na, na, na, na, na, na, na, na). Don't it feel like:

(Na, na, na, na, na, na, na, na, na, na, na, na, na, na).

CAN'T SLEEP LOVE

Words and Music by AVRIEL KAPLAN,
KEVIN OLUSOLA, KIRSTIN MALDONADO,
MITCHELL GRASSI, SCOTT HOYING,
KEVIN FIGUEIREDO, TEDDY PENA,
ELOF LOELV and WILLIAM WELLS

SING

Words and Music by MITCHELL GRASSI,
SCOTT HOYING, KEVIN OLUSOLA,
MARTIN JOHNSON and SAM HOLLANDER

D.S. al Coda

MISBEHAVIN'

Words and Music by MITCHELL GRASSI,
SCOTT HOYING, MATTHEW RADOSEVICH
and RUTH ANNE CUNNINGHAM

Is it stu - pid that I'm ask - ing, "Do you miss me?"

Are you be - hav - ing? 'Cause I'm sav -

- ing all my love _____ for you. ___ And

I'm hav - ing a good time, but I'd rath - er be with you. ___

REF

Words and Music by KEVIN OLUSOLA,
SCOTT HOYING and TAYLOR PARKS

FIRST THINGS FIRST

Words and Music by KEVIN OLUSOLA,
SCOTT HOYING and KEVIN FISHER

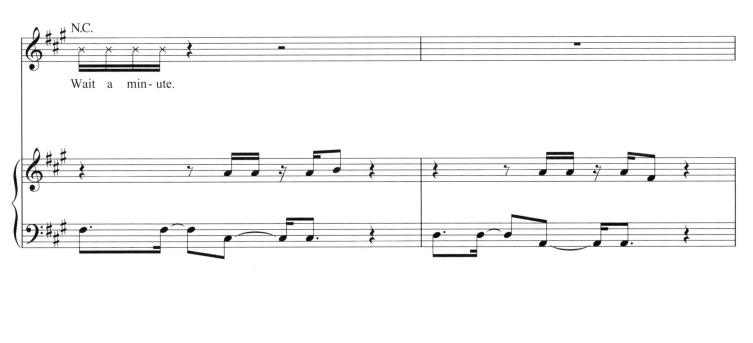

ROSE GOLD

Words and Music by AVRIEL KAPLAN,
SCOTT HOYING, ANDREW PEARSON
and STEPHEN WRABEL

Lyrics:
oh, _____ oh, oh. _____
oh, _____ oh,

oh. _____

Like a myth, the sto-ry of our lives could-n't fit in

on-ly black and white, _____ -ite. _____

clas - sic, we could be stars, we could be rose gold, _____

rose gold. _____

We could be dia - monds, we could be an an - them, we could be

stars, we could be rose gold, _____ rose

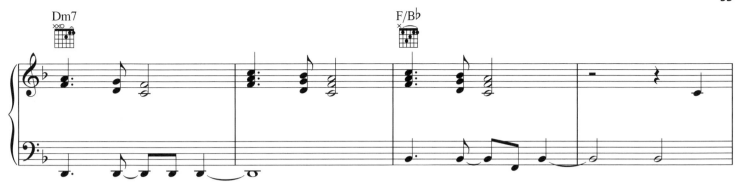

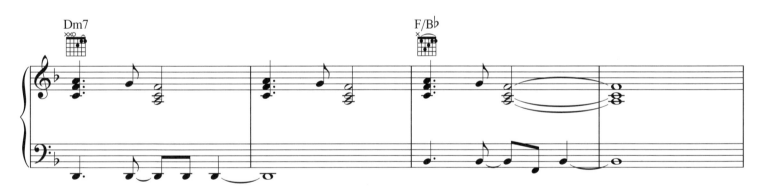

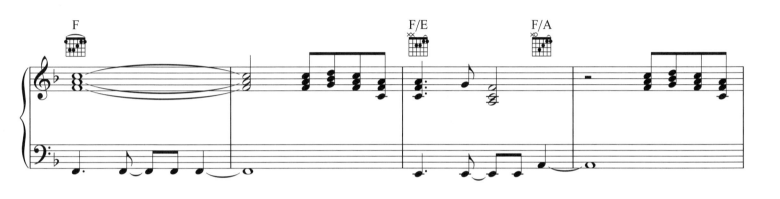

We could be time - less, we could be class - ic, we could be

IF I EVER FALL IN LOVE

Words and Music by
CARL MARTIN

Moderately

(Ooh, da - da doo, doo, doo. Ooh, da - da doo, doo, doo.

Ooh, da - da doo, doo, doo. Ooh, da - da, da - dap.) The ver - y first

time that I saw your brown eyes, your lips said "Hel - lo" and I said "Hi." ___

CRACKED

Words and Music by AVRIEL KAPLAN,
SCOTT HOYING, TALAY RILEY
and CHRISTOPHER J. BARAN

WATER

Words and Music by KEVIN OLUSOLA,
KIRSTIN MALDONADO and AUDRA MAE

Could I tell ____ you ____ this time ____ how I wish

you were mine? ____

My voice _ cracks, ____ I wait for it to pass; ____

heart beats ____ fast _____ with words I can't take ____ back.

TAKE ME HOME

Words and Music by KEVIN OLUSOLA,
KIRSTIN MALDONADO and AUDRA MAE

NEW YEARS DAY

Words and Music by MITCHELL GRASSI,
SCOTT HOYING, KEVIN OLUSOLA
and SAM HOLLANDER

To- night the ap - ple falls _ in time. We'll

sing a - long _ with "Auld _ Lang Syne" _ and throw con-fet - ti high _ up in - to space. _

LIGHT IN THE HALLWAY

Words and Music by MITCHELL GRASSI,
SCOTT HOYING and AUDRA MAE

Close your eyes, lay your head down. Now it's time to sleep. May you find great ad - ven - ture

WHERE ARE U NOW

Words and Music by SONNY MOORE,
THOMAS PENTZ, JASON BOYD,
KARL RUBIN BRUTUS, JUSTIN BIEBER
and JORDAN WARE

CHEERLEADER

Words and Music by OMAR PASLEY,
MARK BRADFORD, CLIFTON DILLON,
SLY DUNBAR and RYAN DILLON

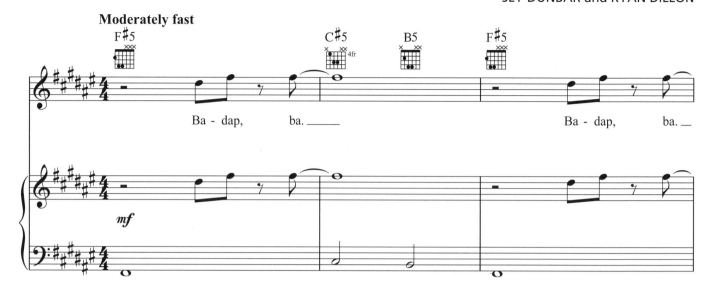

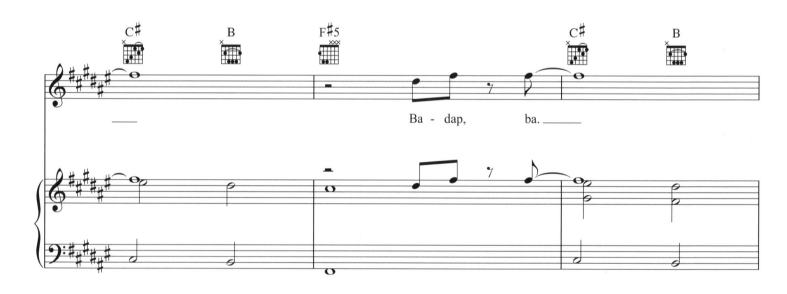

LEAN ON

Words and Music by KAREN MARIE ÃRSTED,
THOMAS PENTZ, WILLIAM GRIGAHCINE,
MARTIN BRESSO and PHILIP MECKSEPER